Fantastic ✷ Physical ✷ Science ✷ Experiments

Jazzy Science Projects with Sound and Music

Robert Gardner

Enslow Elementary

an imprint of

Enslow Publishers, Inc.

40 Industrial Road	PO Box 38
Box 398	Aldershot
Berkeley Heights, NJ 07922	Hants GU12 6BP
USA	UK

http://www.enslow.com

Enslow Elementary, an imprint of Enslow Publishers, Inc.

Enslow Elementary® is a registered trademark of Enslow Publishers, Inc.

Library of Congress Cataloging-in-Publication Data

Gardner, Robert, 1929–
    Jazzy science projects with sound and music / Robert Gardner.—1st ed.
      p. cm. — (Fantastic physical science experiments)
    Includes index.
    ISBN 0-7660-2588-8 (hardcover)
    1. Sound—Experiments—Juvenile literature. I. Title. II. Series
    QC225.5.G37 2006
    534'.078—dc22

                              2005018729

Printed in the United States of America

10 9 8 7 6 5 4 3 2 1

Illustration credits: Tom LaBaff

Cover illustration: Tom LaBaff

Contents

(Experiments with a 🏅 symbol feature **Ideas for Your Science Fair**.)

Introduction

This book is filled with experiments about sound and music. Doing experiments will help you understand how sounds are made and how sound travels. You will learn how to make musical notes, how we hear, and much more.

Entering a Science Fair

Some experiments in this book (those marked with a 🎗 symbol) have ideas for science fair projects. However, judges at science fairs like experiments that are creative, so do not simply copy an experiment in this book. Expand on one of the ideas suggested or develop a project of your own. Choose something you really like and want to know more about. It will be more interesting to you, and it can lead to a creative experiment that you plan and carry out.

Before entering a science fair, read one or more of the books listed under Further Reading. They will give you helpful hints and lots of useful information about science fairs.

Safety First

To do experiments safely, always follow these rules:

1. Do experiments under adult supervision.

2. Read all instructions carefully. If you have questions, check with the adult.

3. Be serious when experimenting. Fooling around can be dangerous to you and to others.

4. Keep the area where you work clean and organized. When you have finished, clean up and put all of your materials away.

5. Never experiment with electric wall outlets.

1. Making Sounds

What makes sound? You can do an experiment to find out!

1 Hold a rigid plastic ruler firmly against a table. Let part of the ruler extend beyond the table. With your other hand, pluck the end of the ruler that can move. Can you hear a sound?

2 How does the sound change if less of the ruler is beyond the table? What happens to the sound if more of the ruler is beyond the table?

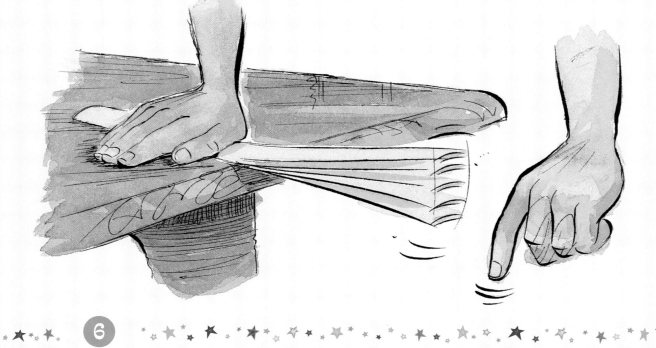

❸ Stretch a rubber band over an opening in an empty box. Pluck the rubber band. What do you hear? What do you notice about the rubber band when it is making a sound?

Things you will need:
✔ rigid plastic ruler
✔ table
✔ rubber band
✔ empty box, such as facial tissue box

❹ What happens to the sound if you stretch the rubber band even more before plucking it?

Making Sounds:

Sounds are made when something vibrates (moves back and forth or up and down). When the ruler moved up and down, you probably heard a sound. When the rubber band vibrated, it also made a sound.

You made the part of the ruler that vibrated shorter. When you did this, the ruler vibrated faster. When you made it longer, it vibrated slower.

When you stretched the rubber band more over the empty box, it vibrated faster.

When something vibrates fast, we hear a sound with a high pitch. It sounds more like a soprano voice. Slower vibrations make a lower pitch, more like a bass voice.

Vibrations have a frequency. Frequency is how many times something moves back and forth (vibrates) in one second. Humans can hear things that vibrate as slowly as 20 times each second and as fast as 20,000 times per second. A dog can hear sounds with frequencies of 15 to 50,000 per second. A dolphin can hear sounds with frequencies as low as 150 and as high as 150,000 vibrations per second.

An Explanation

high pitch (high frequency)

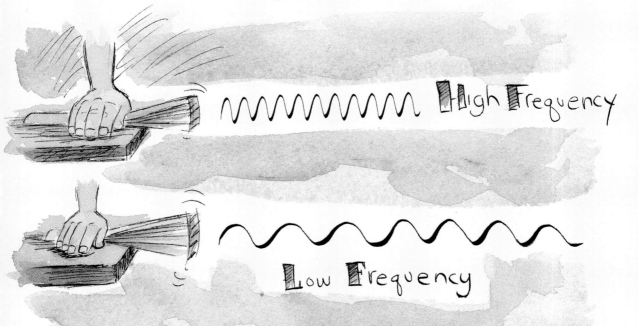

High Frequency

Low Frequency

low pitch (low frequency)

Ideas for Your Science Fair

★ Use a "silent" dog whistle to show that dogs can hear sounds beyond the range of human hearing.

★ Design experiments to measure the hearing range for different animals.

2. Feeling Sound

Can you feel the vibrations made by sounds? Do an experiment to find out!

Let's Begin!

Things you will need:
- ✔ radio
- ✔ large balloon
- ✔ twistie
- ✔ plastic wrap
- ✔ empty oatmeal (or similar) box
- ✔ rubber band
- ✔ salt
- ✔ cooking pot
- ✔ spoon

❶ Tune a radio to a station playing music. Turn up the volume.

❷ Blow up a large balloon. Seal its neck with a twistie. Hold the balloon with the fingertips of both hands. Put the balloon against the radio's speaker. Can you feel the sound vibrations with your fingers?

❸ Can you feel the sound vibrations made by your voice? To find out, hold the balloon with your fingertips. Place it close to your mouth. Then sing a song or speak loudly. Can you feel the vibrations?

❹ Hold the balloon with your fingertips. Sing a low note. Then sing a high note. What is different about the feel of the notes?

5 See the effects of sound vibrations. Stretch a piece of plastic wrap over the open end of an empty oatmeal box. Use a rubber band to keep it tightly stretched. Sprinkle some salt on the plastic. Hold a cooking pot upside down over the plastic. Hit the bottom of the pot with a spoon. What happens to the salt grains?

6 How do the salt grains react to other sounds?

pot

salt on plastic wrap

oatmeal container

Feeling Sound:

In Experiment 1 you found that vibrations cause sounds. In this experiment you felt the vibrations. Sound vibrations made by voices, radios, musical instruments, and other sources of sound move through air. Sound vibrations made air inside the balloon vibrate. You could feel the vibrations. You could probably feel that the high-pitched sounds had a higher frequency than the low-pitched sounds.

You made sounds above the stretched plastic wrap. The sound vibrations traveled through air. The air vibrating against the plastic made the plastic vibrate. The vibrating plastic made the salt grains move.

You probably noticed that loud sounds made the salt move more than softer sounds. Louder sounds make bigger vibrations.

Sound vibrations travel through air to your eardrum. The vibrating air makes your eardrum vibrate. Your eardrum is attached to tiny bones that vibrate. The bones make a fluid inside the inner ear vibrate. The fluid excites a nerve in the inner ear.

An Explanation

The nerve carries signals to your brain, where you "hear" the sound.

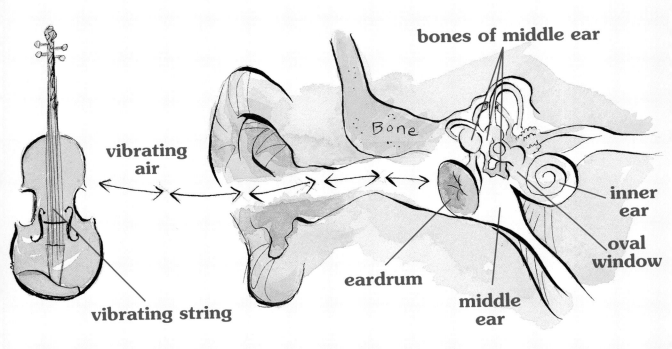

bones of middle ear

Bone

vibrating air

vibrating string

eardrum

middle ear

inner ear

oval window

Ideas for Your Science Fair

★ Make a working model of the human ear to show how we hear sounds.
★ Make up experiments of your own that allow you to feel sounds.

3. Sound Through Air

You can do an experiment to see how sound travels through air.

Things you will need:
- ✔ an adult
- ✔ light above a kitchen sink
- ✔ kitchen sink
- ✔ water
- ✔ matches
- ✔ candle
- ✔ empty 1-gallon plastic milk jug
- ✔ heavy spoon
- ✔ level table
- ✔ grooved ruler
- ✔ 6 identical marbles

❶ **Ask an adult** to turn on a light over a kitchen sink. Fill the sink with about an inch of water. Dip your finger into the center of the water. Watch the wave move. See how it bounces back (reflects) when it hits the side of the sink.

❷ Dip your finger again and again. Watch the waves. This motion is similar to how sound waves from a vibrating object move through air.

❸ See what a single pulse of air can do! **Ask an adult** to light a candle. Hold an empty one-gallon plastic milk jug about a foot from the flame. Point its mouth at the flame. Bang hard on the bottom of the jug with a heavy spoon. Why do you think the flame goes out?

❹ See how sound moves through air. Put a grooved ruler on a level table. Place six identical marbles on the ruler. The marbles represent molecules of air. Pull one marble to the side. Give it a push like the push an air molecule gets from a vibrating object. When it hits the next marble, what happens? How do you think sound moves through air?

about 1 foot

Sound Through Air:

The movement of sound waves through air is similar to waves traveling through water. (The waves are different, though: Sound waves move air together and apart; water waves move up and down.) The waves you made with your finger moved outward to the sides of the sink. (You could see the bright images of the waves on the bottom of the sink.) These waves were reflected toward the center of the sink. When you hear an echo, it is because sound waves have been reflected.

You made a big pulse of air when you hit the milk carton. The single vibration of the bottom of the carton pushed air outward. The air pulse was strong enough to put out a flame. A musical instrument's vibrating string does the same thing to air over and over again, but with much less force.

You pushed one marble into the others. Each marble, in turn, pushed the next one. In the same way, air molecules carry sound away from a vibrating object. A vibrating object pushes air molecules together each time it vibrates. These compressed (squashed) bands of air move away as

An Explanation

sound waves at a speed of about 340 meters per second (760 miles per hour).

vibrating string

Idea for Your Science Fair

★ Use a Slinky spring toy to show how a sound wave travels. Then use it to show how a water wave travels.

4. Sound Through Solids

Sound travels through air. Can it travel through solids?

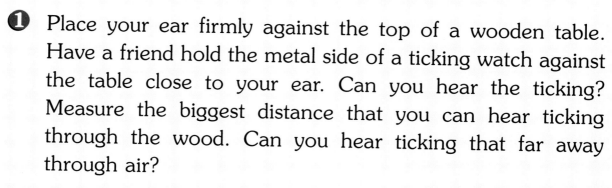

Let's Begin!

1 Place your ear firmly against the top of a wooden table. Have a friend hold the metal side of a ticking watch against the table close to your ear. Can you hear the ticking? Measure the biggest distance that you can hear ticking through the wood. Can you hear ticking that far away through air?

2 Hold the side of a drinking glass firmly against one ear. Hold the metal side of the watch firmly against the other side of the glass. Does sound travel through glass?

3 Repeat the experiment using an empty soda can instead of a glass. Does sound travel through metal?

4 Hold the handle of a metal dinner fork with your thumb and finger. Tap the tines gently with a dinner knife. Quickly hold the fork tines near your ear. You should hear a ringing sound.

5 Now hold the fork handle between your teeth. Again, tap the tines **gently** with a dinner knife. What do you notice?

tick

trck

tick

tick

trck

trck

wooden table

watch

tick tick tick trck

trck tick trck tick

Sound Through Solids:

With your ear against the wooden table, you heard the ticking very well. In fact, you could hear it through wood farther away than through air. Sound travels better and faster through wood than through air. You probably found that sound travels very well through glass and metal, too.

You heard the vibrating tines better with the dinner fork between your teeth. The sound was carried to your inner ear by the bones in your head. Like other solids, bones carry sound very well.

Sounds goes faster through solids than through air. That is because the molecules of solids are very close together. The molecules of air are far apart. Sound moves from molecule to molecule. If the molecules are close together, sound can travel faster. The molecules do not have to move far before bumping their neighbors.

The following table gives the speed of sound in different kinds of matter.

An Explanation

Substance	Speed of sound in substance in		
	meters per second	feet per second	miles per hour
vacuum*	0	0	0
carbon dioxide	270	886	604
air	340	1,115	760
hydrogen	1,320	4,330	2,950
water	1,470	4,820	3,290
glass	5,000	16,400	11,180
iron	5,120	16,790	11,450

*Sound must have matter to travel on. There are no sounds in the vacuum of outer space, where there is no matter.

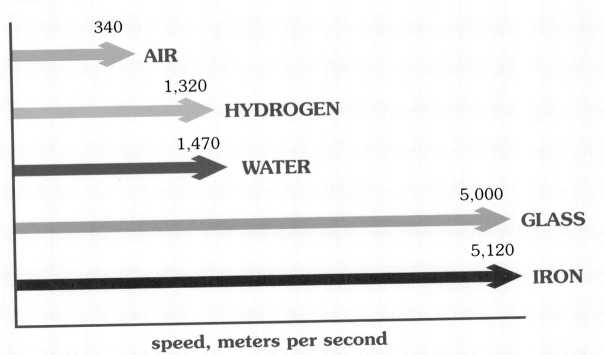

speed, meters per second

5. Are Two Ears Better

Things you will need:
- ✔ large room
- ✔ chair
- ✔ a helper
- ✔ blindfold of dark cloth
- ✔ radio
- ✔ rubber hose about 1.5 meters (4–5 feet) long
- ✔ marking pen
- ✔ ruler

1 Place a chair in the middle of a large room. Have a helper sit in the chair. Blindfold the helper. Keep the blindfold on the helper during the entire experiment.

2 Stand about 1 meter (several feet) away from the chair. Clap your hands and ask your helper to point to the sound. Repeat at different places around the chair. Can your helper point to the sounds you make?

3 Have your helper cover one ear firmly with his hand. Repeat the experiment. Does he find it more difficult to locate sounds with one ear?

4 Turn on a radio and repeat the experiment. Is he less able to locate the sound of your clapping when there are other sounds?

5 Find a piece of rubber hose about 1.5 meters (4–5 feet) long. Mark the center of the hose. Place the hose behind your helper. Have him hold the ends of the hose against his ears. Scratch the tube at various places with your fingernail. Can your helper tell whether the sound is coming from the right or the left side of the hose? At what distance from center can he tell right from left?

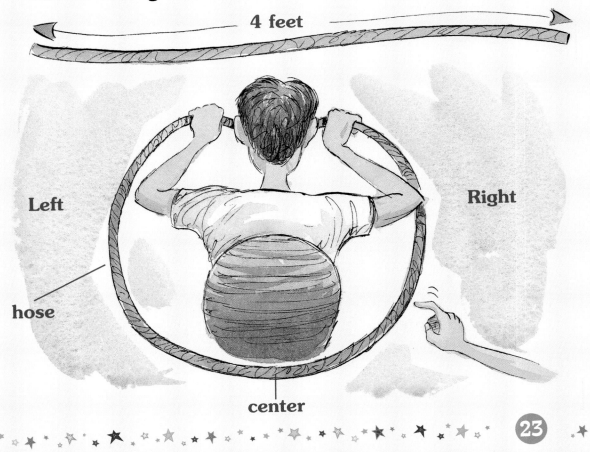

4 feet

Left

Right

hose

center

Are Two Ears Better Than

With two ears, most people can locate sounds quite well. There are clues. Sounds are louder in the ear nearer the sound. Also, the sound reaches the nearer ear a little sooner than the other ear.

louder, shorter distance

less loud, longer distance

With only one ear, it is more difficult to locate sounds. The clues used with two ears are no longer present.

Your helper was probably less able to locate sounds when the radio was on. He heard several sounds at the same time. This made it hard to concentrate on just one sound.

One? An Explanation

Many animals have muscles that allow them to move their ears. They can turn their ears toward a sound. This helps them hear better. It also helps them locate the direction from which sounds are coming.

Some people can move their ears, too. Can you?

Is that a can opener calling?

Ideas for Your Science Fair

★ Make a variety of "telephones" using string, tin cans, a hose, and other household items. Which "telephone" works the best?

★ Does cupping your hand behind your ear help you to hear better? If so, why?

6. Thickness, Length, and

1 Find two rubber bands that are about the same size. One should be thick, the other thin.

2 Stretch the rubber bands over an open, empty box, such as a shoe box or tissue box.

3 Pluck the thick rubber band. Then pluck the thin one. Which has a higher pitch (frequency)? How does thickness affect a rubber band's frequency of vibration?

Pitch

④ Find two tongue depressors, coffee stirrers, or craft sticks. Place them side by side on the edge of a table or counter. Let one stick out farther than the other. Use one hand to hold them firmly in place with a block of wood.

Things you will need:
- ✔ 2 rubber bands about the same size; 1 thick, 1 thin
- ✔ open, empty box (facial tissue box or shoe box)
- ✔ 2 tongue depressors, coffee stirrers, or craft sticks
- ✔ table or counter
- ✔ wood block

⑤ With your other hand, pluck the long one. Then pluck the short one. Which one has the higher pitch (frequency)? What happens if you make them longer? Shorter? How did the length of the stick affect its pitch or frequency?

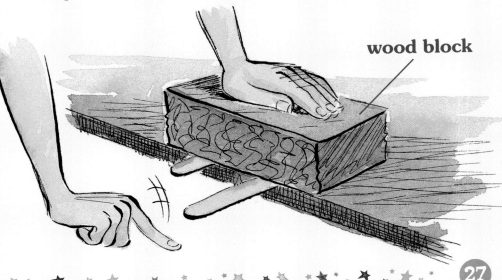

wood block

Thickness, Length, and

You probably discovered that plucking the thinner rubber band made a higher pitch (higher, more soprano-like sound). Since it had a higher pitch, it must have vibrated faster. It had a greater frequency. The thicker rubber band had a lower pitch. It vibrated more slowly. It had a lower frequency.

The same is true of stringed musical instruments. A thick guitar string vibrates slower than a thinner one of the same length. The thick string makes a sound with a lower pitch than a thinner string. A thicker rubber band or string is heavier. Heavy things are harder to move. Given the same push, a lighter object moves faster than a heavier one.

You plucked the wooden sticks. The shorter one made a higher-pitched sound than the longer one. The same is true of vibrating strings. To make a violin string vibrate faster, the musician shortens the string. She does this by pressing a point along the string against the fingerboard. Then only a section of the string vibrates—the part she plucks or bows.

Pitch: An Explanation

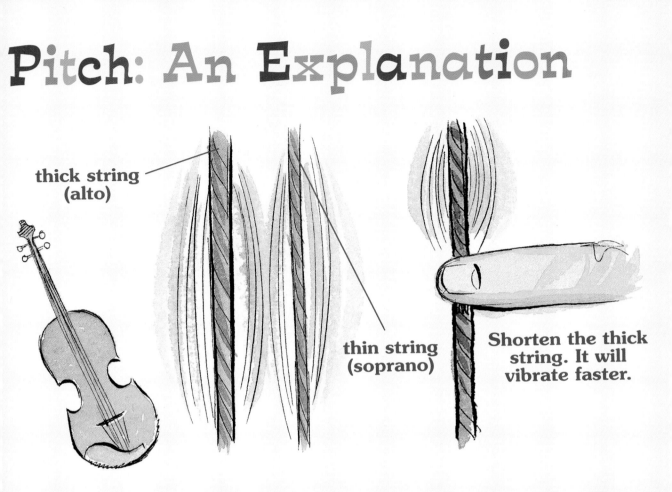

thick string
(alto)

thin string
(soprano)

Shorten the thick
string. It will
vibrate faster.

Ideas for Your Science Fair

* Find eight tongue depressors or craft sticks. Use them to build a simple musical instrument on which you can play tunes.
* Examine a variety of stringed musical instruments. Notice the difference in thickness of the strings. Talk to the musicians who play them. How do the musicians make sounds with different frequencies?

7. Tension and Pitch

Pulling on a string stretches it. The pull (force) on the string is called tension. Does tension affect vibration frequency (pitch)?

Let's Begin!

❶ **Ask an adult** to find or cut a board (2 inches x 4 inches x 2 feet). Hammer a nail into the board near one end. Place the board on a table.

❷ Using scissors, cut a 3-foot length of fishing line. Tie one end to the nail. Tie the other end to a plastic pail. Let the pail hang over the end of the board opposite the nail.

❸ Fasten the board to the table with a C-clamp. Put a tongue depressor on edge under the fishing line near the nail.

❹ Pour a quart of water into the pail. This puts tension on the line. Pluck the line and listen.

❺ Add another quart of water. Pluck the line again. How does more tension affect the vibration frequency (pitch) of the line?

6 Put a second tongue depressor under the line near the other end of the board. Pluck the line between the two tongue depressors. The line will vibrate. To change the length of the vibrating line, move the second tongue depressor. How does the length of a string affect its vibration frequency?

Things you will need:
- ✔ an adult
- ✔ board, 2 in x 4 in x 2 ft
- ✔ nail
- ✔ hammer
- ✔ table
- ✔ cover for table
- ✔ scissors
- ✔ ruler
- ✔ monofilament fishing line, 20–50 pound test
- ✔ plastic pail
- ✔ 3– or 4–inch C-clamp
- ✔ 2 tongue depressors
- ✔ measuring cup
- ✔ water

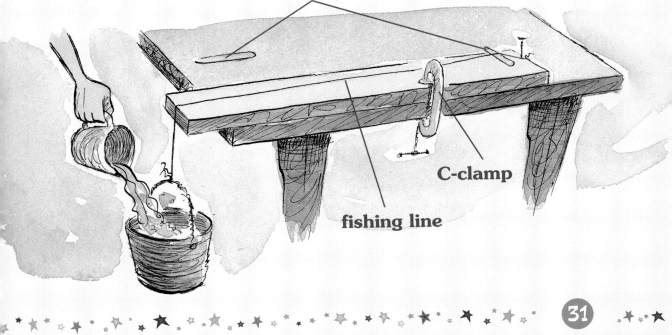

tongue depressors

C-clamp

fishing line

Tension and Pitch:

You probably discovered that increasing the tension on a line (string) raises its pitch. The line vibrates faster, with a greater frequency.

In Experiment 6, you found that shortening the tongue depressor made it vibrate with a higher frequency. When plucked, its pitch was higher than the pitch of a longer tongue depressor. The same is true of a string under tension.

You made the string shorter or longer by moving the second tongue depressor. When you made it shorter, its pitch was higher. It had a greater frequency. When you made it longer, its pitch was lower. Its frequency was less.

A violinist adjusts the tension on his instrument's string to get the right pitch. He does this by turning a tuning peg, which changes the tension on the string. Increasing tension makes it vibrate faster, with a greater frequency.

He can also make the string shorter by pressing it against the fingerboard. The shorter string will vibrate with a higher frequency. The note played will have a higher pitch.

An Explanation

strings

tuning pegs

chin rest

fingerboard

bridge

Idea for Your Science Fair

★ Change the board and string you used in this experiment into a one-string banjo. Use the banjo to play simple tunes such as "Mary Had a Little Lamb," "Row, Row, Row Your Boat," "Jingle Bells," and others.

8. Matching Vibrations

Vibrating things have a natural frequency. The middle-C string on a piano vibrates 261.6 times per second when struck. That is its natural frequency. Suppose that same frequency is sung or played on another instrument. The piano string will vibrate to the matching frequency. You can learn more about matching frequencies by doing an experiment.

Let's Begin!

Things you will need:
✔ 2 empty, clean, 1-liter plastic soda bottles
✔ a friend
✔ 1 empty, clean, 2-liter plastic soda bottle

❶ Hold your lower lip against the edge of the mouth of an empty 1-liter plastic soda bottle. Blow into the bottle. You should hear a low-pitched sound. The sound is caused by air vibrating in the bottle.

❷ Hold the same bottle next to your ear. Have a friend stand in front of you and blow into an identical bottle. What do you hear coming from your bottle? What does your friend hear when you blow into your bottle?

❸ Repeat the experiment, but have your friend blow into a 2-liter plastic bottle. Listen with a 1-liter bottle. What is different this time? How do the sounds made with the 1-liter and 2-liter bottles differ?

What kinds of musical instruments use vibrating air to make sounds?

Matching Vibrations:

When you blew into the 1-liter bottle, the air in it vibrated. It vibrated at its natural frequency, which had a low pitch. When your friend blew into an identical bottle, the sound traveled to the bottle next to your ear. The natural frequency of the air in the two bottles was the same. The air in the second bottle was pushed back and forth at its natural frequency, so it produced the same sound (the same frequency). Its sound was not as loud because its air was not pushed as hard.

The larger 2-L bottle had a different natural frequency. You heard it make a sound with a lower pitch. Its natural frequency did not match that of the smaller bottle. The air in the smaller bottle was not pushed back and forth at its natural frequency. It made no sound.

Musical instruments known as woodwinds (flute, clarinet, saxophone, and others) and brasses (trumpet, French horn, trombone, tuba, and others) produce sounds by making air vibrate. To produce different notes, they change the length of the airway

An Explanation

in the instrument. This causes the air inside to vibrate at different frequencies.

Ideas for Your Science Fair

- ★ Make a musical instrument that produces sounds when you make the air in it vibrate.
- ★ Sing notes toward the strings of a piano. Why may more than one string vibrate?

9. Glassy Tunes

Y ou can make a musical "instrument" and play some simple tunes.

❶ Line up 5 to 8 drinking glasses. (With 8 you may be able to play a full musical scale—do, re, mi, fa, so, la, ti, do.)

❷ Put a small amount of water in one glass. Nearly fill another identical glass. Tap each glass gently with a spoon. Which glass produces the higher note? Can you explain why?

❸ Fill all the glasses to different levels with water. Adjust the levels until you can play simple tunes by gently tapping the glasses with a spoon.

❹ If you find it difficult to tune the glasses, ask someone with a good ear for music to help you. Then try to play some simple tunes such as "Mary Had a Little Lamb," "Bah, Bah, Black Sheep," "Row, Row, Row Your Boat," "Jingle Bells," and others.

❺ Try to write, play, and sing some songs of your own.

Glassy Tunes:

To produce a high-pitched note, you put just a little water in the glass. Putting more water in a glass lowered the pitch. Glasses of different thicknesses and heights produced notes with different frequencies.

Adding water to a glass made it heavier, so it produced a note with a lower pitch. In Experiment 6, you found that thick, heavy strings or rubber bands vibrated slower than lighter ones. They had a lower pitch than thinner, lighter ones. Heavy things are harder to move. Given the same push, a lighter object vibrates faster than a heavier one. As you have discovered, the same is true of drinking glasses.

Thin-walled wineglasses can be shattered by a note from an opera singer's voice. This happens if the note being sung is loud and matches the natural frequency of the wineglass.

An Explanation

A heavier string vibrates slower than a lighter string.

A heavier glass vibrates slower than a lighter glass.

10. More Fun with Sound

There are lots of other fun things you can do with sound. Making sound effects is one of them.

 Let's Begin!

① Sound effects are used in plays, movies, and TV shows. Try making some sound effects of your own. For example, you can make a squeaking door sound. Hold a Styrofoam cup firmly in place. Put the mouth of another Styrofoam cup inside the first one at an angle. Then slowly turn the second one.

② Crinkle some stiff cellophane paper. It sounds like a crackling wood fire. Crinkling softer cellophane sounds like bacon frying in a pan.

③ Move paper cups across one another in various ways. You can make the sound of horses walking, trotting, or galloping.

④ Design and produce some sound effects of your own.

⑤ Use a voice recorder to record a variety of everyday sounds—a dog drinking, water running into a bathtub, rain falling on a roof, a cell phone ringing, and so on.

Play the sounds back. Can your friends and family identify the sounds?

6 Record your own voice and the voices of your friends and family. Which voice does not seem familiar? Why?

Squeeeeeeeeak

HUGO

More Fun with Sound:

How does a sound effect work? It makes a sound with the same frequency as the sound it imitates. You turned the mouth of a Styrofoam cup inside an identical cup. The sounds made by the cups rubbing together have certain frequencies. These frequencies match those of squeaky door hinges.

Usually, we see the source of a sound at the same time we hear it. Some people find it difficult to identify a sound without other clues. They need to see or feel its source when they hear it. For that reason, some people may not be able to identify the sounds you recorded.

You probably found it difficult to recognize a recording of your own voice. Normally you hear voices when the sound travels through air to your ears. The sound of your own voice travels through bone as well as air to your middle ear. This gives the sound a different quality. In addition, muscles in your ear reduce the loudness of your own voice. When you hear your recorded voice, the sound travels only through the air.

An Explanation

Words to Know

force—A push or a pull.

frequency—The number of times something vibrates in one second.

hearing range—The frequencies, from lowest to highest, of sounds that can be heard. The hearing range of humans is from 20 to 20,000 vibrations per second.

molecule—The smallest particle of a substance that can exist by itself. Molecules are very small. A drop of water contains more than a billion trillion molecules.

natural frequency—The number of times that something, such as a string, normally vibrates because of its length, thickness, and tension.

pitch—The number of vibrations heard per second. The higher the pitch, the greater the number of sound vibrations per second.

solid—Anything that has a definite shape and size.

sound—A vibration that moves through air or other matter.

speed—The distance something goes during a certain time. A car might have a speed of 60 kilometers per hour (38 miles per hour). Sound travels through air at a speed of approximately 1,220 kilometers per hour (760 miles per hour).

tension—A force trying to stretch something, such as the pull on the string of a musical instrument.

vibration—Any back-and-forth motion, such as the motion of a plucked violin string.

Further Reading

Bombaugh, Ruth. *Science Fair Success, Revised and Expanded*. Springfield, N.J.: Enslow Publishers, Inc., 1999.

Cobb, Vicki. *Bangs and Twangs: Science Fun with Sound*. Brookfield, Conn.: Millbrook Press, 2000.

Levine, Shar, and Leslie Johnstone. *Science Experiments with Sound & Music*. New York: Sterling Publishing Co., Inc., 2002.

Nankivell-Aston, Sally, and Dorothy Jackson. *Science Experiments with Sound*. Scholastic Library Publishing Co., 2000.

Parker, Steve. *Sound*. Broomall, Pa.: Chelsea House Publishers, 2005.

Searle, Bobbi. *Sound*. Brookfield, Conn.: Millbrook Press, 2002.

Internet Addresses

Exploratorium, the Museum of Science, Art and Human Perception. *The Science of Music*.
<http://www.exploratorium.edu/>

The Franklin Institute Online.
<http://sln.fi.edu/>

Scifair.org, and John W. Gudenas. *The Ultimate Science Fair Resource*. © 2000.
<http://www.scifair.org>

Index